70/1580S

The Organist in Season

Summer

Compiled by Gilbert M. Martin

Cover Design: Janine Chambers
Editor: Gilbert M. Martin
Engraver: Lani Smith

ISBN: 978-0-89328-329-2

THE SACRED MUSIC PRESS

Box 802, Dayton, Ohio 45401-0802
www.lorenz.com

Foreword

Completing our remarkable series of compilations of seasonal organ music, we proudly present our Summer volume, culled from the broad and diverse library of The Sacred Music Press. Fourteen exceptional settings of service music shine out, highlighting the celebration of the Holy Trinity, the rite of Holy Communion, appropriate selections for Home and Family, and even something special for a Patriotic Sunday. Rounding out the collection are three general praise and four general prayer hymn arrangements. All timings are accurate and the indices are organized alphabetically, by page number and by the church year. Under any circumstance, a most desirable and prestigious addition to the organist's library.

—The Publisher

Contents

Please see page 48 for an alphabetical index and the back cover for an index organized by Church Year.

Ye Watchers and Ye Holy Ones

Hw. Bourdon 16, Offenflöte 8, Octav 4, *mf*
Pos. Flutes 8, 4, 2 [Scharff], *mf*
Ped. Trumpet 8 [c.f.] (or Solo Reed 4, played one octave lower than written)
   On one manual:
Hw. Flute 8, Octav 4
Ped. Trumpet 8

Gerhard Krapf
Tune: **LASST UNS ERFREUEN**, *from*
Geistliche Kirkengesäng, *Köln, 1623*

Duration: 3:30

LS

6

Dove of Peace
~ I Come With Joy ~

Sw. Soft 8, 4
Gt. Solo stop or combination
Ped. Soft 16, 8

Gilbert M. Martin
From The Southern Harmony, *1835*

Duration: 2:15

www.lorenz.com

LS

For C. Griffith Bratt

Antiphonal Paraphrase on "Lobe den Herren"

I   Full, without Reeds
II   Flutes 8, 4, 2, Light Mixtures
III   Reed 8
Ped. Principals 16, 8, 4, Trumpet 8

David A. Wehr
Tune from Erneuerten Gesangbuch, *Stralsund, 1665*

Duration: 2:30

O Master, Let Me Walk with Thee

Sw. Flute 8, 4
Gt. Reed 8
Ped. Bourdon 16, 8, 4

Paul Karvonen
Tune: **MARYTON,**
by Henry P. Smith

Duration: 1:30

www.lorenz.com

LS

Chorale Prelude on "Duke Street"

Gt.   Full without Reeds
Ped. *f* 16, 8

Robert J. Powell
Tune by John Hatton, 1793

Duration: 2:15

Variations on "America"
I. Tune

Sw.   Principals
Gt.   Principals, Reeds

Austin C. Lovelace
Based on "Thesaurus Musicus,"
London, ca. 1740

Duration: :45

II. Mirror Canon

Sw.   Krummhorn 8
Gt.   Flute 8, 4

Duration: :45

III. Poco Allegro

poco staccato

Duration: :45

IV. Poco Adagio

Sw. Strings and Celeste

Duration: :45

*Sharp is optional.

V. Toccata

Full Organ
Ped. Full, plus Reeds

Duration: 1:00

SACRED
Keyboard & Instrumental Collections

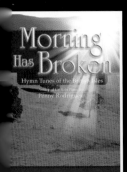

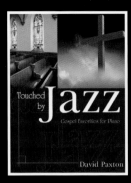
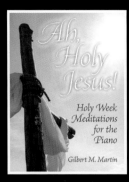

PIANO
General

MORNING HAS BROKEN
Hymn Tunes of the British Isles
Penny Rodriguez
70/1591L • $12.95
Incorporating ten traditional hymn tunes from the British Isles, Penny Rodriguez lends her personal pianistic style to nine fresh settings for the church pianist. Though well crafted and fully realized, these appealing vignettes have an improvisatory nature and allow ample latitude for the performer to apply a personal interpretive imprint. The ultimate result, however, is a musically satisfying presentation of some of the most beloved melodies from the rich heritage of hymnody from Great Britain. Moderately easy to medium difficulty.

Lord, Enthroned in Heavenly Splendor (BRYN CALFARIA)
Immortal, Invisible/Let All Things Now Living
(ST. DENIO and ASH GROVE)
Today We All Are Called to Be Disciples (KINGSFOLD)
Morning Has Broken (BUNESSAN)
The King of Love My Shepherd Is (ST. COLUMBIA)
Jesus Shall Reign (DUKE STREET)
All Through the Night (AR HYD Y NOS)
I Sing the Mighty Power of God (FOREST GREEN)
The Lord My Shepherd Guards Me Well (BROTHER JAMES' AIR)

AN OFFERING
Expressions of Worship for Solo Piano
Bethany K. Smith
70/1587L • $15.00
From the pen of this young, innovative church pianist come ten fresh and creative arrangements of well-loved hymns and meditations. Each setting is artistically sculpted to blend well into any worship service setting. The musical styles, varied from easy to moderate levels of difficulty, range from quiet, peaceful settings to more energetic, high-spirited praise offerings. Regardless of the styles, these well-crafted expressions of worship will be a blessing to pianists and congregations alike.

An Offering • Come Thou Fount! • 'Tis So Sweet
Be Thou My Vision • Prelude on a Traditional Welsh Hymn
Give Me Jesus • Redemption • The River • Coronation
It Is Well

RESURRECTION SUITE
Vibrant Hymn Settings for Piano
Mark Hayes
70/1592L • $12.50
This is piano writing from Mark Hayes that you've come to know and love...creative harmonies, interesting modulations, orchestral flourishes, dramatic mood shifts, all in playable arrangements that fit comfortably under the fingers. Perfect for general use or Eastertide, this trio of resurrection songs for solo piano will help you celebrate the risen Christ. Consider using the arrangements as a prelude, offertory and postlude, either separately or as a suite. Medium to advanced difficulty.

Crown Him with Many Crowns
Look, Ye Saints! The Sight Is Glorious! • Thine Is the Glory

TOUCHED BY JAZZ
Gospel Favorites for Piano
David Paxton
70/1589L • $12.95
Touched by the warm, lush harmonies of the jazz idiom, these ten gospel gems are given an endearing new sparkle by the deft compositional hand of David Paxton. Improvisatory in nature, fresh in spirit, and embued with many "oh, that's nice" moments, these tastefully crafted settings are a joy to play and hear.

I Am Thine, O Lord • I'll Go Where You Want Me to Go
There Is a Fountain • Redeemed • Oh, How I Love Jesus
'Tis So Sweet to Trust in Jesus • I Hear Thy Welcome Voice
I Must Tell Jesus • The Everlasting Arms
Will There Be Any Stars in My Crown?

Eastertide

AH, HOLY JESUS!
Holy Week Meditations for the Piano
Gilbert M. Martin
70/1552S • $15.00
This colorful and beautifully realized anthology of familiar piano hymn settings will enhance your Holy Week celebration, highlighting that special time of penitence and sacrifice, meditation and contemplation, prayer and remembrance. These gentle, graceful and warm arrangements, all accurately timed, reflect the retrospective quality of this remarkable time for the Christian soul.

Go to Dark Gethsemane (REDHEAD)
Alas! And Did My Savior Bleed? (MARTYRDOM)
There Is a Green Hill Far Away (HORSLEY and MEDITATION)
In the Cross of Christ I Glory (RATHBUN)
Beneath the Cross of Jesus (ST. CHRISTOPHER)
Ah, Holy Jesus! (HERZLIEBESTER JESU)

WHAT WONDROUS LOVE!
Lenten Meditations and Easter Celebrations for Piano
Larry Shackley
70/1593L • $12.95
Lent, Palm Sunday and Easter are all well represented in this striking compendium of seasonal settings for piano. Larry Shackley is fast becoming one of the premiere composers for the church today, and this collection of artistically crafted hymn settings will only augment and enhance his well-deserved growing reputation.

Wondrous Love • Beneath the Cross of Jesus
Grace Greater Than Our Sin • All Glory, Laud and Honor
God So Loved the World (from *The Crucifixion* by John Stainer)
Christ Arose • Jesus Lives, and So Shall I
The Day of Resurrection

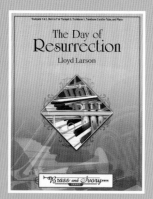
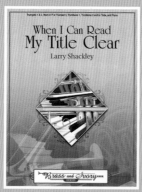
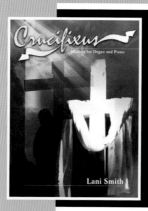

INSTRUMENTAL

The Brass and Ivory Series

Built around a brass quintet nucleus with piano accompaniment, this series is designed to provide practical yet creative resources for church musicians. The arrangements in this series are crafted by some of today's leading arrangers, and they are worthy considerations for preludes, offertories and general service music. Accessible for most church, school and community brass ensembles.

THE DAY OF RESURRECTION
(Lead On, O King Eternal)
Lloyd Larson
30/2209L • $15.95
Tune: LANCASHIRE
Trumpets 1 & 2, F Horn or Trumpet 3, Trombone 1, Trombone 2 and/or Tuba, and Piano

WHEN I CAN READ MY TITLE CLEAR
Larry Shackley
30/2206L • $15.95
Tune: PISGAH
Trumpets 1 & 2, F Horn or Trumpet 3, Trombone 1, Trombone 2 and/or Tuba, and Piano

Also Available:

WEDDING SUITE FOR BRASS QUINTET
Lloyd Larson
30/2084L • $19.95
2 Trumpets, F Horn, Trombone and Tuba

Joyful, Joyful, We Adore Thee (prelude)
Canon in D by Pachelbel (attendant processional)
Processional (bridal processional)
Savior, Like a Shepherd Lead Us (service music)
Recessional (bridal party recessional)

ORGAN & PIANO

Eastertide

CRUCIFIXUS
Medleys for Organ and Piano
Lani Smith
Three-staff • 70/1588L • $15.00
Thirteen evocative hymns of the cross have been skillfully melded into four medleys focusing on different aspects of the sacrifice of Jesus. Created by a master of the genre, these medleys feature both instruments equally, using the idiosyncratic sonorities of each. Useful from Lent through Eastertide, each medley will stir the soul and instill the appropriate sensibility for the congregation to be especially attuned to both personal and corporate modes of worship. Two copies are required for performance.

The Suffering Savior: HERZLIEBSTER JESU, WERE YOU THERE and WONDROUS LOVE
The Cross: MARTYRDOM, ST. CHRISTOPHER and RATHBUN
The Sacrifice: GETHSEMANE, PASSION CHORALE and MEDITATION
The Redemption: RHOSYMEDRE, THE SOLID ROCK, WOODWORTH, and HAMBURG

ORGAN

General

EASY ORGAN LIBRARY
Volume 41
Two-staff • 70/1601L • $18.00
Just beginning? Trying to make the leap from piano to organ? Looking to refresh your repertoire without committing to hours of practice? This ninety-six page, spiral-bound collection of preludes, offertories and postludes, printed on two staves and reprinted from *The Organist*, is the perfect resource for all of those circumstances and countless others. Registrations are provided for all organs and durations are provided to aid programming decisions.

THE ORGANIST IN SEASON: SUMMER
Compiled by Gilbert M. Martin
Three-staff • 70/1580S • $18.00
Completing our remarkable series of compilations of seasonal organ music, we proudly present our Summer volume, culled from the broad and diverse library of The Sacred Music Press. Fourteen exceptional settings of service music shine brightly, highlighting the celebration of the Holy Trinity, the rite of Holy Communion, appropriate selections for Home and Family, and even something special for a Patriotic Sunday. Rounding out the collection are three general praise and four general prayer hymn arrangements. All timings are accurate and the indices are organized alphabetically, by page number and by the church year. Under any circumstance, a most desirable and prestigious addition to the organist's library.

Ye Watchers and Ye Holy Ones (LASST UNS ERFREUEN)
Dove of Peace (I COME WITH JOY)
Antiphonal Paraphrase on "Lobe den Herren"
O Master, Let Me Walk with Thee (MARYTON)
Chorale Prelude on "Duke Street" • Variations on "America"
For the Beauty of the Earth (DIX) • Ricercare on "St. Anne"
This Is My Father's World (TERRA BEATA)
Dear Lord and Father of Mankind (REST)
Bread of the World in Mercy Broken (RENDEZ À DIEU)
Prelude on "King of Love" (VATER UNSER)
All Things Bright and Beautiful (ROYAL OAK) • Brother James' Air

 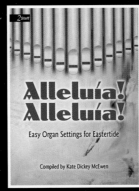 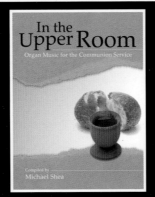 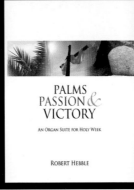 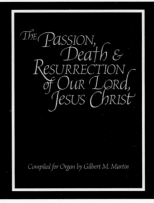

THE ORGANIST'S LIBRARY
Volume 41
Three-staff • 70/1602L • $18.00
Whether you are adding another volume to your collection or just starting your library, this set of moderately challenging classics, hymn fantasies and choral preludes, reprinted from *The Organ Portfolio*, is a must-have for every church organist. Ninety-six pages and spiral bound, the music is printed on three staves in an upright format with registrations provided for all organs. Durations are also included to aid programming decisions.

Eastertide

ALLELUIA! ALLELUIA!
Easy Organ Settings for Eastertide
Compiled by Kate Dickey McEwen
Two-staff • 70/1594L • $15.00
The liturgical season from Easter to Trinity Sunday is a significant period in the life of the church, but it can often present programming challenges for even the most gifted organist. Here, organized by church year, is a collection of skillfully arranged hymn tunes for Easter, Post-Easter, Ascension, Pentecost, Transfiguration, and Trinity Sunday. These fourteen selections range from bold, powerful arrangements to quiet, contemplative pieces, but all will be a welcome addition to your post-Easter worship services.

Jesus Christ Is Risen Today (LLANFAIR)
Rejoice, the Lord Is King! (DARWALL'S 148TH)
Low In the Grave He Lay (CHRIST AROSE)
Love Divine, All Loves Excelling (BEECHER) • Nothing But the Blood (PLAINFIELD)
On Christ the Solid Rock I Stand (SOLID ROCK) • Jesus Shall Reign (DUKE STREET)
All Hail the Power of Jesus' Name (DIADEM, CORONATION, MILES LANE)
Holy Spirit, Truth Divine (MERCY)
Come, Gracious Spirit, Heavenly Dove (MENDON)
Fill Me Now • Christ, Whose Glory Fills the Skies (RATISBON)
All Creatures of Our God and King (LASST UNS ERFREUEN)
Come, Thou Almighty King (ITALIAN HYMN)

IN THE UPPER ROOM
Organ Music for the Communion Service
Compiled by Michael Shea
Three-staff • 70/1595L • $15.00
In response to many requests, we proudly present this stunning collection of organ music that beautifully complements the meditative qualities of the communion service. The opening selection, *The Last Supper* by John Innes, sets the gentle mood for the entire volume. There are fourteen prayerful and reverent pieces included, six of which are familiar hymn settings, plus four masterful arrangements from the classic repertoire. All of the music is quite accessible, accurately timed and registered for all organs.

The Last Supper *(Innes)* • Sweet Hour of Prayer *(Hughes)*
Cantilena *(Rheinberger)* • Hear My Song, O Lord *(Southbridge)*
Meditation on "Gordon" *(Peterson)* • I Call to Thee, Lord Jesus Christ *(Bach)*
Bread of the World *(Martin)* • In The Upper Room *(Broughton)*
Breath from a Bounteous Heaven *(Southbridge)* • Adagio *(Grieg)*
My Faith Has Found a Resting Place *(Southbridge)*
Here, O My Lord *(Paxton)* • Cleansing Fountain *(Broughton)*
Cantabile *(Guilmant)*

PALMS, PASSION AND VICTORY
An Organ Suite for Holy Week
Robert Hebble
Three-staff • 70/1582S • $15.00
From the pen of one of America's great organist/composers comes this notable and finely wrought suite for Holy Week. Imaginative and breathtaking in its challenging scope, the composer offers new musical insight and inspiration to the great hymn tunes ST. THEODULPH and RATHBUN. His joyous postlude of Easter praise is a bristly and punctuated amalgamation of EASTER HYMN, VICTORY and ST. KEVIN.

All Glory, Laud and Honor (ST. THEODULPH)
In the Cross of Christ I Glory (RATHBUN)
Christ the Lord Is Risen Today (EASTER HYMN, VICTORY and ST. KEVIN)

THE PASSION, DEATH & RESURRECTION OF OUR LORD, JESUS CHRIST
Compiled by Gilbert M. Martin
Three-staff • 70/1581S • $18.00
The worshipful week from Palm Sunday (or Passion Sunday as it is often called) to Easter Sunday is abundant with opportunities for special music in the life of the church, and this vibrant compilation of organ music is especially tailored for that purpose. These twelve settings, many of which are based on favorite congregational hymn tunes, celebrate the excitement of Jesus' entry into Jerusalem, his final moments with his disciples in the Upper Room, his harrowing crucifixion, and his triumphant and glorious resurrection. A dramatic and eloquently artistic collection for the enrichment of this important Christian experience.

Improvisation for Palm Sunday (VALET WILL ICH DIR GEBEN)
Prelude on "When Jesus Wept" • Carillon • Hosanna! Hosanna!
Were You There When They Crucified My Lord? (WERE YOU THERE?)
Fantasy Prelude on an Easter Hymn (CHRIST IST ERSTANDEN)
At the Lamb's High Feast We Sing (SONNE DER GERECHTIGKEIT)
The Old Rugged Cross (OLD RUGGED CROSS)
Jesus Christ Is Risen Today (EASTER HYMN)
Christ Hath Burst His Prison! (ST. KEVIN)
Come to Calvary's Holy Mountain (ALBERT)
O Saving Victim, Opening Wide the Gate of Heaven (O SALUTARIS HOSTIA)

How To Order ...

To order any of these collections, please contact your favorite music supplier or visit www.lorenz.com for a list of dealers near you.

All prices are in U.S. dollars and subject to change without notice.

Trinity/Pentecost

ORGAN MUSIC FOR THE TRINITY SEASON
Gerhard Krapf
Three-staff • 70/1577S • $15.00

The longest season of the church year, Trinity begins eight weeks after Easter and continues until Advent, nearly half of the calendar year. And with many Christian hymns fitting these many Sundays, this prominent and venerable composer has crafted a copious and delightful collection of sixteen organ settings appropriate for the Trinity season. Useful as separate preludes, offertories and postludes within the worship service, or even as hymn introductions, they will find an important place in the organist's library.

Holy, Holy, Holy! Lord God Almighty! (NICAEA)
Alleluia! Sing to Jesus (HYFRYDOL)
O Word of God Incarnate (MUNICH)
Praise to the Lord, the Almighty (LOBE DEN HERREN)
Sing Praise to God, the Highest Good (LOBE GOTT DEN HERREN, IHR)
Jesus Lives! The Victory's Won! (JESUS, MEINE ZUVERSICHT)
When I Suffer Pains and Losses (WARUM SOLLT ICH MICH DENN GRÄMEN)
Grant, Holy Ghost, that We Behold (ES IST GEWISSLICH)
Father Most Holy (CHRISTE SANCTORUM)
O That I Had a Thousand Voices (O DASS ICH TAUSEND ZUNGEN HÄTTE)
O Sing, My Soul, Your Maker's Praise (WÄCHTERLIED)
Out of the Depths I Cry to You (AUS TIEFER NOT)
Open Now Your Gates of Beauty (UNSER HERRSCHER) • Trumpet Tune
Sing to the Lord of Harvest (WIE LIEBLICH IST DER MAIEN)
Lord, Keep Us Steadfast in Your Word (ERHALT UNS, HERR)

PENTECOST SUITE
A Hymn-based Trilogy for Organ
David Cherwien
Three-staff • 70/1579S • $15.00

For Pentecost, that great festival which marks the birth of the Christian church by the power of the Holy Spirit, three glorious hymns have been magically arranged for organ by this well-known and respected composer. Perfect as a prelude, offertory and postlude, or separately as a concert suite, a dance-like O HEILGER GEIST, a mysteriously floating DOWN AMPNEY and a fiery, roof-rattling VENI, CREATOR SPIRITUS will thrill your congregation. A glorious addition to the organ repertoire, speaking as it does to this special, sanctified celebration.

O Spirit of Life (O HEILIGER GEIST)
Come Down, O Love Divine (DOWN AMPNEY)
Come, Holy Ghost, Our Souls Inspire (VENI, CREATOR SPIRITUS)

Wedding

EASY STANDARD WEDDING MUSIC FOR ORGAN
Compiled by James Southbridge
Two-staff • 70/1590L • $15.00

Here—as requested by many—is the 2-staff edition of our consistent and long-time best-seller, Standard Wedding Music for Organ (70/1550L). Like the first book, this compilation is divided into two sections for ease of use: section one serves as a resource for the prelude, and section two provides a variety of well-known processional and recessional options. All of the pieces included have certainly earned the status of "standard," and it is with joy that we make them available for all organists.

"Air" from the D Major Suite *(Bach)* • Peaceful Prayer *(Curtis)*
"Allegro" from Sinfonia No. 12 *(Vivaldi)*
"Allegro Vivace" from *Water Music (Handel)*
Canon in D *(Pachelbel)* • If Thou Art Near *(Bach)*
Jesu, Joy of Man's Desiring *(Bach)* • Largo *(Vivaldi)*
Morning Has Broken *(arr. Broughton)* • Dove of Peace *(arr. Martin)*
"Andante Grazioso" from Sonata in A Major *(Mozart)*
Panis Angelicus *(Franck)* • Träumerei *(Schumann)*
Bridal Chorus from *Lohengrin (Wagner)*
"Festal March" from *Rinaldo (Handel)*
Prelude in Classic Style *(Young)* • Hymn to Joy *(Beethoven)*
"With Trumpets and Horns" from *Water Music (Handel)*
Processional for a Joyful Day *(Wood)* • Trumpet Tune *(Purcell)*
Wedding March *(Mendelssohn)* • Trumpet Voluntary *(Clarke)*

STANDARD WEDDING MUSIC FOR ORGAN
Compiled and Edited by David Sarandon
Three-staff • 70/1550L • $15.00

The dictionary describes standard as "something used as a measure, a norm, or an agreed level of attainment." This collection, then, is aptly titled, as each of the pieces included have certainly earned the status of standard. The compilation is divided into two sections for ease of use: Section One serves as a resource for the prelude and Section Two provides a variety of processional and recessional options.

Partial list of contents:
"Allegro" from Sinfonia #12 *(Vivaldi)*
"Andante Grazioso" from the A Major Sonata *(Mozart)*
Canon in D *(Pachelbel)* • If Thou Art Near *(Bach)*
"Largo" from Guitar Concerto *(Vivaldi)*
Traumerie and Romanze *(Schumann)*
Bridal Chorus *(Wagner)*
"Festal March" from Rinaldo *(Handel)*
Processional for a Joyful Day *(D. Wood)*
Wedding March *(Mendelssohn)*
With Trumpets and Horns *(Handel)*

Lorenz Publishing Company   THE SACRED MUSIC PRESS   Exaltation
                                                         The Lorenz Corporation

**To order, contact your favorite music supplier or
contact The Lorenz Corporation for a dealer near you.
www.lorenz.com**

AD657   P.O. Box 802, Dayton, OH 45401-0802

For the Beauty of the Earth

Sw.   Flute 8, Principal 4
Ch.   Cornet (8, 4, 2, 2 2/3, 1 3/5)
Ped. 16, 8, Sw. to Ped.

Alec Wyton
Tune: **DIX**,
by Conrad Kocher, 1838

Duration: 2:00

www.lorenz.com   LS

Ricercare on "St. Anne"

Sw. Full
Gt. Full
Ch. Full
Ped. Full

Gordon Young
Tune attr. to William Croft, 1708

Duration: 1:45

This Is My Father's World

Gilbert M. Martin
Tune: **TERRA BEATA,**
by Franklin Sheppard

Sw. Soft Flute 8
Gt. Solo Flute 8
Ped. Flutes 16, 8

Duration: 2:00

70/1580S-32

www.lorenz.com

LS

Dear Lord and Father of Mankind

Sw. Oboe
Gt.   Soft Strings
Ped. 16, 8

Albin C. Whitworth, ASCAP
Tune: **REST (ELTON)**,
by Frederick C. Maker

Duration: 3:00

LS

With movement ♩ = ca. 69

Bread of the World in Mercy Broken

Sw. Principal 4
Gt.   Flute 4
Ch. Flute Celeste 8
Ped. Sw. to Ped. 8

Emma Lou Diemer
Tune: **RENDEZ À DIEU**,
by Louis Bourgeois, c. 1510-1561

Duration: 3:45

www.lorenz.com

LS

rit.

-Sw. to Ped.
+Gt. to Ped.

Prelude on "King of Love"

Sw.   Soft Solo Reed 8
Gt.   8, 4, *mp*
Ped. 16, 8, uncoupled (or +Gt. to Sw.)

Raymond H. Haan
Tune: **VATER UNSER,** *from*
V. Schumann's Geistliche Lieder, *1539*

Duration: 2:30

All Things Bright and Beautiful

Sw.   Light Reed 8
Gt.   Flutes 8, 2
Ch.   Light 8, Flute 4
Ped. Bourdon 16, 8 (uncoupled)

Dale Wood
Tune: **ROYAL OAK,**
English, 17th cent.

Duration: 1:45

Brother James' Air

Sw. String, Flute Celeste 8, 4
Gt. Light Reed 8
Ped. Soft 16, 8

Gilbert M. Martin
Based on the tune
by J. L. Macbeth Bain (c. 1840-1925)

Duration: 2:45

LS

Alphabetical Index